Taste The Bright Moment

Poems from Cheshire, Shropshire
and Staffordshire

Taste The Bright Moment

Poems from Cheshire, Shropshire
and Staffordshire

An anthology from
Keele Poets at Silverdale

First published by The Coracle, December 2024
4 Derwent Close, Alsager, Cheshire ST7 2UT
Tel: 01270 882060 email: PhilWilliams441@gmail.com

ISBNs pbk 978-1-0685464-0-2
       ebk 978-1-0685464-1-9

Copyright © 2024 belongs to the authors

No part of this publication may be reproduced, stored in a retrieval system, or transmitted, in any form or by any means mechanical, electronic, photocopying, recording or otherwise without the prior written consent of the publisher; nor be otherwise circulated in any form of binding or cover other than that in which it is published and without a similar condition being imposed on the subsequent purchaser.

The right of each poet to be identified as the author of their work has been asserted by them in accordance with the Copyright, Designs and Patents Act 1988.

Cover illustration by Ryan Derricutt
Typesetting www.ShakspeareEditorial.org

Being With Writers

You learn to taste the bright moment,
discover a fox's nose, a buzzard's focus,
a delicate ear subtle as the owl's flight.
Maybe touch green alchemy.
Being with writers you unearth the ways of apples,
how they ripen and swell, and then let go.

Annabel Wade

Contents

Introduction	1
Hilary Adams	3
Envoi	3
From Peak District Haiku Project	3
Bed Time Stories	4
Melanie Amri	6
Rubbish	6
Graeme Barrie	7
You Showed Me Sapphire Dreams	7
The Wrong Road	7
Ferry Castle, Sunday Morning	8
Should Auld Acquaintance Be Forgot	9
Roger Bradley	10
Yorkshire Sculpture Park 11/11/2019	10
When We Were Gods	11
Rosemary Brough	12
Letting It Go	12
The Terrace, Penkhull	13
View Of Delft	14
Pause At The Threshold	14
Mary Dale	16
Afternoon Tea	16
For Angela	17
Christmas Eve Radio	18
National Distrust	18
Janet Fielding	19
Haiku	19
Tracey Greenhough	20
Time Goes By	20
Caroline Hawkridge	21
Peregrine	21
Cockerel	23
Saqqara	24
Roger Hill	25
Beyond The Roaches	25
Winter Diamonds	26

Miranda Howle — 27
  The Wardrobe — 27
  Sunlit Moments — 27
Mark Johnson — 28
  A Trouble Shared — 28
  Flow Gently … — 28
Helen Kay — 29
  1940 Manchester Blitz — 29
  Friday Afternoons Are Different Now — 29
  Lighting The Wood Stove Six Months After Your Death — 30
  Stomach — 31
Mary King — 32
  My Father's Apron — 32
  Praise To Water — 33
  I Lost My Four Front Teeth — 34
  What I See Out Of My Window These Days — 35
Maurice Leyland — 36
  Bonding — 36
  Lighter Than Air — 37
Derek Matthews — 38
  Scotched — 38
  Haiku — 39
Bill Milner — 40
  Home — 40
  The Garden — 40
Bert Molsom — 41
  Reclining Figure In Elmwood — 41
  The Ashes — 42
Harry Owen — 43
  A Kind Of Life — 43
  Message From Astbury Mere — 43
  Roadside Festive — 44
Ian Malcolm Parr — 45
  Names On The Wall — 45
  Angels In The Hedgerows — 46
Karen Schofield — 47
  Hope Valley — 47
  Junior Doctor Learning Log — 48
  Myeloma Moths — 49
  Relativity At The Midnight Matinee — 49

John Smith	**50**
Tick All The Boxes	50
John Statham	**52**
Wake For Brown	52
Not Waving	52
Betty Titley	**54**
To A Brother	54
Partings	55
Megan Smith	**56**
Undercurrent	56
Another Place	56
Talking Of Socks	57
Forever	58
Annabel Wade	**59**
Gannets Off Port Soy	59
Child	60
Kintsugi	60
Scottish Image	61
Mary Williams	**62**
Pickling Onions	62
Tracklements (A Lancashire Memory)	63
Philip Williams	**64**
Uniform	64
Perennials	65
Red Triangle	66
One Long Summer	67
Acknowledgements	**68**

Introduction

'Some things have their own signs' – and others are 'perennial'.

You are reading a collection of poems by a group of writers whose talent goes before them and which spans several decades. The group began life as an adult education class at Keele University, back when there was funding for such things. When the funds dried up, it continued to meet at Silverdale Library with a succession of tutors, of whom I am the latest and least. It is rather like Doctor Who. Every so often the tutor / facilitator 'regenerates' and turns into somebody else. Previous tutors include Caroline Hawkridge and the first Cheshire Poet Laureate Harry Owen. I feel privileged to follow in their footsteps and to know, and have known, such a great set of people.

Several members remain from those early days and new folk have joined. We miss those who have passed away or who have moved on. I am grateful to the relatives of those who are no longer with us for granting permission to reproduce some of their work here. I hope you will agree that there is a great range and variety of work, some in traditional forms, others in free verse, some witty, some poignant, all intriguing. The group has changed over the years of course, but it retains its distinguishing features – friendliness, warmth and a love of words.

Some poems have appeared previously, in one or other of the three *Keele Haul* collections, in the authors' own publications, in poetry journals or online. I have provided credits and acknowledgements where this is the case.

This is the second poetry publication from 'The Coracle'. The first, *Petrol & Matches* was an anthology of poems from The Nantwich Words & Music Festival competition between 2013 and 2017. It is hoped to produce further publications featuring poems from Keele Poets at Silverdale and other groups around the region.

I would like to thank the volunteers and staff at Silverdale Library, particularly for their forbearance. It is not every day that an absent-minded poet takes their toilet key home! I would also like to thank the group for their patience, in particular Graeme Barrie and Karen Schofield for forming a small editorial and selection team. Any omissions or mistakes are purely my own.

Read on, enjoy the company of writers and 'taste the bright moment'.

Philip Williams
The Coracle, November 2024

Hilary Adams

Envoi
A Scarcity of T-Shirts

Never climbed the Himalayas,
led a demo, asked to guest
on a television chat show,
never conquered Everest
never rode a bucking Bronco,
caught a salmon, panned for gold,
never dropped by parachute or
abseiled down Big Ben. I'm old
now – too late to try a skateboard,
keep a lobster for a pet:
never been there, never done that,
never got the T-shirt. Yet,
looking back I've had my moments,
facing challenges galore;
though old age is far from humdrum,
don't want T-shirts any more.

From Peak District Haiku Project

Laughing grandchildren
leap through Swythamley bracken,
being wallabies.

Surely poets named
Cloud, Wildboarclough, Shining Tor,
Windgather, Wincle?

Peek District
Showering naked
I see distant Shutlingsloe,
but can it spot me?

Bed Time Stories
1

Do you remember that couple we met
on the bridge above ... Coniston was it?
or maybe Loweswater? Their daughter played bridge

rather well ... Isobel? or Marie, was she?
No matter. But he
reminded me so much of James
Thing ... you know, the bald man
we heard sing in that musical play
we saw at the Haymarket.

What were they called,
the people we met on our wet
honeymoon break in the Lakes?

Both began with a B...
Was it Brenda? Belinda and Bob
Berisford? Billington? Blunkett?
It's right on the tip of my tongue...
yes, surely her mother
was poorly, the doctor called in,
put all the hotel in a spin.

Or was that the inn
where, after a jar
(or two, quite a few),
which you swore you didn't intend,
you'll no doubt recall your fall
from a stool in the bar?

Never mind, I'll be kind
and pretend I've forgotten it all.

2

Yes, of course I remember our honeymoon break
in the Lakes. How could I forget?
April was it, or May? Anyway,
on that first day, miserably wet,
when we struggled to Skiddaw in mist
a watery sun broke through at last –
and we kissed.

But from then on things went downhill fast –
those Burlingtons hove into sight:
Beatrice and Ben they were called
(you're right, he was bald),
with that girl, Isobel in a pet,
looking glum, as she very well might,
soaking wet. Little fool wouldn't wear a cagoule.

And as I recall,
Bea's dreadful old mum,
pigging out on the curry that night,
got distressingly tight,
so the doctor was called in a hurry
for what proved to be nothing but wind…
and we looked at each other and grinned.

So no wonder we went to that inn.
You can think what you like,
but I needed a drink –
or two. So did you.
I even remember my fall, I fear
I've a better memory than you,
my dear. However,
in spite of the weather, or words that were said,
here we are, still together, in bed.

Melanie Amri

Rubbish

Litter is human blossom,
urban potpourri.
It falls from our fingers like a benediction,
transforming dull pavements
into canvases of joy.
We drop it with love,
as a token of our affection
for the world.
Gaze now at those paper bags
floating past vast tower blocks,
like angels borne aloft
for our delectation.
Or see them caught in winter trees –
huge confetti silhouetted against the sky.
Is that not pretty, is that not fine?
Is it not wonderful to watch
coffee cup lids windsurf
across a smooth station floor?
Is there not beauty in a crushed can
as it spins and scrapes?
And how else would we notice
the patterns the wind makes
in city corners, when a gust whips
wrappers against the wall.
Litter is the ultimate democracy –
free and available to all.

Graeme Barrie

You Showed Me Sapphire Dreams

We ran into dancehalls, chased by frantic light,
down wide boulevards in a neon night,
through spinning bottles and overturned cups,
as if the dead-end streets belonged to us.
We held each other in smoke-filled rooms,
laughing lunches lingered through afternoons
into moonlight with bottles drunk, glass by glass,
burning the world until love slept at last.
We talked to each other lying head to toe,
long into the night, about beauty, art and war
and in the dawn, you showed me sapphire dreams
where our whispers kissed and words overflowed,
and as a red sun crawled over the city streets,
we danced so close that you were in my bones.

The Wrong Road

We have been dropped at the foot of a glen,
abandoned, with greasy skin and ragged hair,
leaning into the deluge, four sheets to the wind,
hail bulleting every stride. All day in the open air
above a dark loch that glowers under broken hills,
we scuttle, tired, high in the steep climb
through thick heather, and capercaillie calls,
feeling the country's sadness soak into our limbs.
And the stars twist and the moon takes hold,
and a scarecrow hangs from a rusty pole,
tied loose around with tired rope,
bandaged with straw, fingers crunched into claws,
its hunchback held askew by chopped up logs.
It guards the wrong place. We have taken the wrong road.

Ferry Castle, Sunday Morning

The pale sky on the horizon crusts
where the castle juts over the river,
its cannons watching the still,
taut lines of the fishermen
on the cockle shelled pier.
Kelp hangs limp and tangled
above the brown water, tarnished stones
and whitewashed wood.
Clouds curl where wet washing
spins in a stippled sky.
A slow wind blows from the west
hugging the bank of the river,
dancing up the low hill where
freshly painted walls and wide open windows
frame faces watching the empty beach
in the lonely sound of gulls.
All that's left in the harbour is
a wooden bridge balanced on stilts,
the skeleton beams of an unfinished boat
and fragments of a tune rumbling
from a red jowled man
who staggers out of The Eagle
and points his face at the lifeboat shed.
It's Frankie Boy, still singing
his Saturday songs in the backyards,
his rough last night falling in on top of him,
his face bandaged in wonder,
his eyes green slits in yellow pouches,
asking for absolution on this Sunday morning.

Should Auld Acquaintance Be Forgot

And we'll beat time on an empty drum,
pass around our last bottle of rum,
sing songs to nights we'll never forget
as a pipe and a fiddle play a lament.
We'll sing the fragile, stolen words
from the saddest song we've ever heard
with the sweetest voice that thrills the night.
And we'll love all this for the rest of our lives,
the four of us dancing along Riverside,
the rhythm of the water taking us home
through the abandoned docks, the golden light
above the bridge bleared in falling snow,
feeling that the stars have come out to die,
and we won't be ashamed to say we cried.

Roger Bradley

Yorkshire Sculpture Park 11/11/2019

Voice over:
    '*Ladies and gentlemen, may we request two minutes
    of silence and reflection on Remembrance Day…*'

Voice inside:
    You poets who write things down,
    there, where the sky is blue again –
    I remember
    the feel of the sun on my back
    before the clouds and rain.
    I remember
    the weight of that rifle
    Dad made for me
    from a piece of wood
    the branch of a tree
    so I could be Buck Jones
    charging around the field.
    I remember
    the bright green field
    the rest of the cowboys
    long before the cap guns
    long before the Lee Enfield…
    See how far it is
    across the grass to the horizon.
    Where I was last,
    that land of mud,
    we could not see the horizon
    just the choking smoke
    but for a moment
    I could remember
    all the boys
    the green field
    the sun on my back …

When We Were Gods

Oh, but we were!
Remember those times
we shot arrows straight up,
watched them vanish ...
All that blue sky!
Watched as they came down ...
No fear. Just kept watching.

But we were gods.
Wanted to be higher, higher
than arrows that fell to earth.
So we climbed The Hills ...

Always late afternoon,
shadow-time, we climbed
when the sun was going
from our small field.

Up, up past the quarry
up the steep paths
to see the Wild, Wild West:
Herefordshire!

A prairie laid out before us.
We were almost touching the sky
as we held our hands up
holding the deepening blue
in its place.

This was our sky!
These were our hills!
A hundred times higher
than our arrows!

Oh yes! We were gods!

Rosemary Brough

Letting It Go

My father had thin lips
and he didn't smile.
I never heard him laugh.
But once, on a Lincolnshire beach,
because the sand stretched on empty for miles,
early-morning smooth,
voluptuous and wet perfect,
he let go.

'Bugger!' he roared up to the sky.
'Damn! Blast! Silly arse!'
And then he yelled all sorts of words
we weren't supposed to hear.

And the five of us joined in,
even my mother
who was carrying the coats,
screeching with the free-wheeling gulls,
'Bugger! Bloody! Sod! Lavatory!'

We went running in zig-zags
flying our arms
swearing
and taking advantage.

The Terrace, Penkhull

The décor is patterned.
There are banquettes. Round tables.
All is arranged with clean, painstaking care.
The wall lights are on.
On this day when it's raining, a hanging lamp
makes a cartwheel of light on the ceiling.

There are no ghosts here,
only real people, feet on the ground,
no liking for exaggeration.
People whose parents had nothing,
now have something,
and lunch out.

The women have tints,
the leisure for pink lacquer,
smart blouses,
and their husband's pleasure
expressed in marcasite and eternity rings.

It's quiet, the *ching* of the till,
small clatter of knives, greetings.
Someone with all the fabric of warmth in her voice
murmurs, 'Ah, the baby. Isn't she lovely?'
and comes, palm up, for the hand
of a tiny, pink girl
lurching on her grandmother's knee,
and slapping her glasses.

There's a small garden, seats.
A view over Stoke, Fenton, Longton.
But today, because of the mist and sitting just here,
these towns disappear,
and all we see are the leaves
and the tops of the trees.

View Of Delft

Vermeer's View of Delft –
heightened inner
projected on outer.
Artist's vision.

And neither does my View exist,
except as an imagined breakfast piece,
an inner place beneath one of his rain-fresh roofs;
an interior
reduced to a soft green corner with a table,
a still life
with a fall of light from the world outside onto
a sliver-thin glass,
a trickle of milk from a jug. A bowl, some bread.
And, as these days I am touched by tablecloths,
some folds of dark plush,
the gleam of starched linen.

Here's no allegory,
just a peaceful housekeeping
made from the shadows and light
passed between a glass, a bowl, two cloths, some bread,
a tranquil trickle of milk.
No narrative at all, yet the mind faced with beauty
will make its endless, wishful story.

Pause At The Threshold

Cloister garden, ready, empty.
At its still centre, a dim rectangle of grass,
the splashing fountain,
and, still half-hidden,
the colonnades' running rhythm.

*

Coffee standing at the window;
sipping, coming to, over the red geranium.
Simple silence. The sky lightening.

*

Sky fills the garth, its grass;
Column, arch, column tunnel light
to rinse the moon inside.

*

Beeswax, leather; closer, sharp smell of print, paper.
A room not to be overawed in,
not to be certain.
Yet let a book be above all other thing:
see, even in your mind, you weigh a book in your hand,
nurse it at the fire;
on the floor sprawl
the colour plates of a folio.

*

Rest your eyes on the peace green turf,
in some inner place, deep enough to lie on.
Meditate the paths, hands in sleeves
pass and pass the leap of a fountain.

*

Homage what you have forged
from dross, what struck from pain:
significant Shanghai silver, Tahiti pearls, and Burma rubies
to fill your walls with gleaming vitrines.
The colonnades throw twilight sun and shadow.
Stand still before the end of the day
that you have hourly walked with thoughts.
Be by the water.

*

Dusk walls. A mat.
A bed. A cotton cover.
And sleep's border.

Mary Dale

Afternoon Tea

'Cirrocumulus,' he says
musing to a mackerel sky
on our daily stroll through Ilkley.

We turn into Bettys.
Fat Rascals and Darjeeling
spread their flavours as
water paint on silk.

The delicate crab
sandwiched, trapped,
shaped by sharp cuts
tastes of risk.
We chew on regardless.

While in the West
the sun burns red,
sinking,
as another crab
crimsons in the pot.

Around us pink tongues
shoot in and out like pistons
steaming through exotic lands:
Welsh rarebit, Swiss torte,
coffee from Ethiopia.

The murmur of money
tinkling porcelain
diamonded fingers
'being Mother', pouring plenty.

At the entrance
a half-gloved hand
serves up *The Big Issue.*
Strong vibrant flavours
crossed off the corporate *à la carte.*

'Let's pay,' he says.
We walk away.
The pianist plays nostalgia,
key to avoiding involvement.

For Angela

Swirling, flirting with my alter egos
windblown russet shadows welcome autumn,
dancing leaves, nature's frisky gigolos
dub me Angela Rippon, I'm awesome.

My lounge becomes a Proscenium Arch,
enter Arachnid stalking the cornice,
her eight elegant legs pace a slow march,
my 'specs steam with fear, my soul a furnace!

My *other* self uses drama and skill,
as Angela I do the mental splits,
coaxing my spider to spin her silk will,
she's not restricted by arthritic hips.

Supple Angela spins down to the floor,
saved by limbo dancing under her door.

Christmas Eve Radio

She sprawls, cat-like, in front of the fire.
Flames lick wood darkness to amber,
spit red lava, burn small craters
in the half-moon rug.

A radio crackles,
announces across the toasted air –
   'we present Richard Burton reading *A Child's Christmas In*
   Wales by Dylan Thomas.'

He sparks her mind
with his chocolate voice, molten, delicious,
flowing from inside the box.

She knew she would save him till last.

National Distrust

Rectangle of scorched summer earth
advertises park litter,
hosts disposable barbecues,
top tat and broken glass,
dangerous detritus
scarring arid grass like acne.

This 'I don't care' graffiti
lurks in lazy wait,

barefooted children

belligerent dogs

septic cuts

third-degree burns

my blazing rage.

Janet Fielding

Haiku

A nip in the air,
Summer, turning the corner,
Slips on fallen leaves.

Relentless rain on
Black-spot blighted sycamore
Beats autumn's tattoo.

Inexorably,
Autumn's blaze flickers and fails.
Dark winter beckons.

Tracey Greenhough

Time Goes By

This photo I see, reveals a time that used to be.
My Mum, could have been a beauty queen,
all flirtatious, with sultry smile.
My Dad couldn't resist those smouldering eyes.
At 18 she had the best of everything,
shy in nature like Princess Di,
so very young, looking for laughter and love.
She sure found that in this funny man, me Dad,
he knew she was the one for him,
off on his motor bike, into the sunset they'd ride.
But I was just a speck of dust,
a hope one day if all goes good,
all wrapped up in these two,
my Mum and Dad so much in love.

Caroline Hawkridge

Peregrine

The blog sings
Four golden plover, three...
then says the cathedral was table
for woodcock
while the country sat down
to turkey.

The bell-tower's peregrines open
the ribs of migrants
all winter. *And a blackbird
on the North side.*

Spring spreads its breast feathers, lets the bald
skin of the sun
brood. The cathedral clock nudges the city
with its long bill. Lenses wait, want
to annunciate.
She will

fidget
four rufous eggs
by the lion-tailed rump of a gargoyle
and several webcam
eyeballs. The nostril in her beak wears the bony
inlet cone of a jet engine. Even sleep is ascent as her lower
  lid rises
to close.
A starling's coverts chequer her ledge.

Its hackles, prized
by fly-dressers for wet flies and flymphs,
were cast. The tiercel keeps surfacing from the bottom
of the city.

He blots
a serif of the new

Taste the Bright Moment

Caroline Hawkridge

letter 'R', the lustre of his feet illuminating the blue
like the idle yellow crane. Only the 'Y' to finish
glass-office minting sky. Here,
again in his gloves: on
a stone finial, police aerial, council roof safety rails, stashing
a corpse in a quatrefoil.
Viewers hatch

their global locations
on the blog, a line of tourists sprockets past the telescope
on the green
below, as he reads
them this city,
leaves

the bloodied bill of a snipe, the silver lobed toes
of a coot taken
to the radio station. She will
feed
the lead gape
of the nave roof its confetti
of feet and beaks.

A world is

asking,
admiring, angry, arguing; the growing clamour
like the oldest ring
of ten bells in England not
deafening the wing-spreading
chicks

crowding
the tower's high pavement, opening
and closing their fledging
umbrellas like spoke-dodging
commuters, until the odd gets
caught, spirals off
the cathedral.

The blog uploads
wing bones fossilised in light;

the wind's angel born
bent. All day,
she will

call.

Cockerel

There you stand: a weather-vane
with one foot held up as if you could pluck
East and West from the very ends
of the earth. You splay
the yellow crackle-glaze of your toes and step
forward, eyeing me with a shiny bit
you might have pecked
from the dust.

The fleshy rinds on your head
make a ramshackle bouquet
when you elongate your neck, part
that kettle beak and start to pour yourself out
and out; the undulating effort travelling
the muscles of your throat as if
you can rouse the world

from its shell of cloud
and molten
yolk.

Saqqara

Horus sees, sees with sun and moon,
his left eye waxing and waning
as falcons are dipped in tar or salted in natron.

Wrapped in linen, bird-masked

and sold in oblong earthen jars,
thousands stack the catacombs;
galleries of potted hawks

in a necropolis of bulls, baboons, ibis
and the swathed mud of faked votives.

Horus sees, sees with sun and moon,

the day eyed with jasper
when a man's heart weighs against the feather:

his arms those of the divine falcon,
his hair strewn,
nostrils inlaid by the wind,

eyebrows two serpents entwined,

lashes firm, coloured with sky,
and his lids, the bringers of peace.

Saqqara: site of an ancient Egyptian animal necropolis.
Horus: falcon-headed Egyptian god of the sky.

Roger Hill

Beyond The Roaches

Go to the moors at the edge of the night
When the sky is gored with the death of the light,
And dark in the valley, the brooding trees
Throb to the tide of a soundless breeze.
Move past the fields where the sheep are stone
And the misty paleness chills to the bone,
And follow the road where the wild rocks lie
Heaped and huge against the sky –
Up to where, in the day's last glow
The crows on their crooked wings are slow,
And the beautiful, shining globeflowers blow
With butter-bright yellow amidst cotton grass snow.
Wait for the strange and soundless owl
To ghost hard by where the hard black fowl
Strut in a wild deep leking rite,
Old when the Druids passed to fight;
And the March hares craze, and the curlew's thrill
Bubbles from every valley and hill …
Aye, go to the moors when life grows bare,
For the ageless pulse of the wind is there.

Winter Diamonds

Today I have gazed upon treasure,
On riches beyond compare:
For the land has been full of diamonds –
Diamonds just everywhere.

They winked from the silver branches
Of every frost-bound tree;
And encased the shimmering white of the snow
With glittering filigree.

Such treasures are not for possessing
And cannot be bought and sold
And those who would reach to grasp them
Will feel only dampness and cold.

Yet they will be there for the asking
As long years wax and wane:
For bright in the memory's precious recall
The diamonds will glitter again.

Miranda Howle

The Wardrobe

I've had a spot of bother with my wardrobe,
It's shrinking things, it's making me fed up.
That pale grey suit which simply cost a fortune
I'm struggling to button or zip up.
When wanting to impress
I'd wear the emerald dress
Now the seams are under stress
Due to bulging bits of flesh.
It's all the ruddy wardrobe's fault, the swine!
As my hats, shoes and gloves still fit just fine.

Sunlit Moments

My mother quoted poetry as others sing a song,
Our lullabies were Wordsworth, Yeats and Tennyson.
Nursery rhymes soon passed, after that rude rhymes
　abounded,
They're still my party piece; love for verse was deeply
　grounded.
How frequently we rose to *The Lake Isle of Innisfree*,
We were Hiawatha's playmates by the shores of Gitchee
　Gumee.
Insidiously, dementia stalked and made her blind
To yesterday: tomorrow could not be – and yet her mind
Recalled lines learnt as a child, she'd smile, her face alight,
As if a glorious shaft of sunlight lit her world of night.

Mark Johnson

A Trouble Shared

It's not been the same since they changed the 503.
And I agreed, making the requisite grimace
while my eyes were fixed on a different bus.

*You never know where you are now. It's all over
the place.* Yes, it *is* a disgrace, I thought –
my Oyster Card at home in the wrong pocket,
the way that man in the queue matches black socks
with alabaster legs. The endless war in Ukraine.

That was probably not what she meant.
But in our shared, not-shared moment
I believe I know the way that she felt.

Flow Gently ...
... *Sweet Afton, Carrols, Woodbine*

These were the soft vapours of my youth
which curled and flowed through my Nan's back room
danced in between radio waves from across
the Irish Sea. Wrapped me safe in a frowsy dream.

Players Navy Cut brought the smack of the Southern Sea,
a man blown through the front door like a Force Ten gale.
He gave me tales of the Merchant Marine, the whaling fleet,
Amundsen, shipwrecks. Left her floundering in the reek
of drink, gambling debts and the corporation rent man not
  paid.

Helen Kay

1940 Manchester Blitz

Mr Seed, next door, hacked the beech hedge
between their houses, to dig a shelter
with a concrete arch nosing into each lawn.
It was only used that one night.

Sipping whiskey, Aunty opens up that
she did not clutch my mother's young hand
but was hysterical by the kitchen sink,
twenty years old and afraid of a hole.

Now vines calm the arch. The new neighbour
has to know, for legal reasons, who owns the
dug out room, they who bought the Seeds' home,
or my aunt, who carries its cold buried truth.

Friday Afternoons Are Different Now

The dental detectorist scans for decay
wants to excavate my mouth, to remove
more bits of me. I decide that he hides
my teeth as trophies in a metal box.
Programmed to hold on to things, I decline
an extraction. Walking to yours I smile past
sprouted tree stumps at the lake.
You walk up and down the tarmac tongue
of a neat close, chat to passing cars.
The chemo has made you gecko.
You say they will keep treating you – for months,
even years, who knows. I lick the rough edge
of my tooth. March clouds hover. We begin
another lap, wobbly, but still biting.

Lighting The Wood Stove Six Months After Your Death

I crumple newspapers from a bundle
you sent me, noosed with baler twine.

As if it knows where it is heading,
a woodlouse rows across war reports,

reaches the crossword. Its antennae tap
the ouija board of your scrawled answers.

The lighter cog clicks its candle glow.
I brood over you and the paradox of fire,

how it can reduce everything to ash,
but here, in the mouth of a stove,

it turns hard news to eloquent warmth.
I close the door to calm the burning.

Stomach

Friday tea. Folds of raw tripe
float in vinegar on her plate,
limp, a bleached coral reef.

Dad pinches out a green Silk Cut.
The cow's body touches his lips.
He swills it down with claggy tea.

Perfect, he spoons out smiles.
Wanting to crayon the white corpse
red, the child eats, forces a swallow.

The blur of work talk drowns her.
She pokes the ash on his saucer,
cuts and cuts the cratered skin.

Years on, she puts her child-self into
a home. When she visits, it hardly
knows her, stares, white and inedible.

Mary King

My Father's Apron

I wear your apron most days,
the one thing I kept,
with all your stains on it.

Brown wax as you sealed leather edges
to shoe us,
last held between your knees.
Mother could never scrub it out.

Bitumen from the fence,
green stuff where you leaned on the shed,
paint spots,
the rooms you painted us.

And it smelt of you;
iron and glue and oil and garden
and bringing the coals in.

Washed by accident,
it was clean.

And it has taken years
of work and wit
and woe and wonder
to get the marks back again.

Praise To Water

'Your depression is due to your insolence and your refusal to praise'.
                Rumi (1207–73)

thirst quencher
diluter

for giving your washing

rinse after rinse
and your hands in it

for the colour of it –
green over sand bars
a depth of blue over coral
the changing greyness
when you are sad
bright shine of holiday

and the sound –
strines and runnels
branches, becks
meres and mountain streams

for the single drop on lady's mantle
tears down the window

for the kind way it curls your hair in rain
as your mother's fingers used to

the swish of car tyres,
your music in the night

the summer swell
of your food plants

the relief of your dog
the glug-gulping relief

the swim of it.

I Lost My Four Front Teeth

I lost my four front teeth on bread and scrape
doled out by ladies with the dripping left
from yesterday's beef roast; then malt extract
in a dessert spoon; then our bottled milk.

And after playtime instruments arrive,
tambourines, Indian bells and one triangle.
Michael who's not all there is given that.
We practice for the Albert Hall.

In the late afternoon the thin and rickety
would sit in vest and pants under UV.
Thus did the LCC attempt to counteract
bad overcrowding, rationing and smog.

Memory's just an historical footnote.
I cross the parquet floor to cast my vote.

What I See Out Of My Window These Days

It's not an aesthetic view.
Rough ground. Cars.
Dead branches. Concrete.

But does that builder's net cry orange
less loudly, than the flame flower
over the roof in next door's garden?

And remembering, when my ears broke –
the first loss, the sound of sparrows,
even the memory – how suddenly
sitting in the kitchen, I heard one calling,
and it was water running
in the machinery of the old fridge.

How it broke itself, to break,
what was broken, in me.

The world comforts
one way or another.

Like someone's conversation
overheard on the train
when you are lonely.

It's me here.
I'm on my way.

Maurice Leyland

Bonding

My hands were small –
skinny fingers, bitten nails,
little latent energy for the task.

Dad's, like knotted twigs,
thick and rough like pitted tarmac,
perfect to grasp, wrench and pull all day.

Our task, to free scraps of coal
from the grip of soil, pebbles, flints,
compacted by rain, and wind and time.

Our need, fuel for our fire,
bunker bare –
since the strike.

The old long-discarded tip,
defunct and valueless,
but not to the desperate.

Several muscle-straining,
Finger-bruising, nail-breaking hours later
Dad said, 'Let's go.'
With our sacked treasure
freed from the grip of the spoil.
we reached our door,
met by Mum with shovel poised.

Lighter Than Air

It must be a dream – I am flying.
Free from the pull of the earth
I lean on the air like a bubble
with no weight or hindrance
to draw me down.

I glance down as the trees shrink,
waver their topmost leaves
in gestures of acceptance of my magnificence.
Godlike I flicker a finger of farewell, causing
my speed to increase towards the nearest cloud

which beckons with tendrils of vapour,
welcoming my exalted presence. I hover
in the tenderness which radiates over my skin
cleansing my thoughts of past and present,
leaving the promise of a limitless future.

Derek Matthews

Scotched

Craggy Skelp is a single malt whisky,
made in the finest Scottish tradition.
It has a strong and smoky intensity
which is unique and irresishtible.
Evry sip of smooth, shweet dishtillation
leaves un afterglow of wharm tinglin taysht.
  Itch alluring an full bodeed flavrin
     ish shtrong an an rich.
         Iss gotta luvly … con … continooity
ana fantashtic finish.
     Leavesja feelin … hic …
        shatishfied.

Haiku

Bottoms Up

Mayfair sewer rats
celebrating their status
were flushed with success.

Russian About

Rushed intelligence
caused the MI5 to be
undermined by a mole.

Pink and Red

The fox which fell foul
of the farmer, chickened out
of pluck at the meet.

An Underlying Situation

The snake couldn't get
a foothold on the ladder
and lost all standing.

Bill Milner

Home

Did war erase your homeland off the map,
destroy your house and then rename your street?
No. Your town is listed in the index still.
Your language and the very way you speak it
are rooted in a certain place and family.
Mine was deemed to be inferior:
too many consonants, the Leader said.
I saw the pit he filled to make the point.

My accent now declares me out of place
and many of the English words I use
bring darkness with them, not your warmth and light:
for me a house is just a house.
Home is through a door inside my head.

The Garden

Our legs are wet from walking through the grass:
the garden they were proud of has run wild.
There was a lawn, some rose beds – and a pond
just deep enough to take away their child.

Bert Molsom

Reclining Figure In Elmwood
Henry Moore 1936

Stripped bare
to show flesh
unseen in the forest.

> *Was I not beautiful*
> *fully clothed*
> *with leaves and bark?*

Felled, to lie full length for impudent pleasure.

> *Trees don't lie down willingly, you know.*

Unmoving
joints are waxed
to enhance the shaping.

> *I am preserved; unable*
> *to return to the ground*
> *and feed others as I should.*

Turned by nature,
in-grained by living.
Metricated by Moore.

> *You say I am cut,*
> *gouged, chopped,*
> *to create a greater beauty.*

Dimensions adjusted
to convert it from natural
to abstract shapes.

> *I say I have been turned*
> *into a shaped suggestion*
> *from an original truth.*

The Ashes

Nothing left
to explain
the ashes,
now cold.
No light,
no heat,
no movement,
no fuel
that had fed the fire.

The dust lies where it should –
returned to its source.
Nothing moves as I walk away.

Harry Owen

A Kind Of Life

For Bill Milner

Bill hasn't posted lately
it says on LinkedIn, which is no surprise
because he died several years ago.
I miss him, fellow poet, translator, friend.

When I knew him, when he knew me, I had
little idea of his importance,
of how fine a writer he truly was.

Perhaps, generous spirit, open mind,
he didn't even know himself.
This then is a reminder to us both.

Message From Astbury Mere

Across a playground of white lined paper,
the nib of an ant: a scribbled note and gone.
Through the vague bloodless blue of evening,
vapour trails slice inscriptions in the sky.

Noise is magnified by water, and here
a quarter mile is howling in my ears
as silently, idly, this brown beetle
alights and, doodling, looks around.

The sudden stiff-legged scrawl of an aphid
prints itself, stilted, crutched, along the margin
and an intrusion of cigarette smoke
hangs in the air. The moon is offended.

How much filth has its eye frowned upon?
Even now its glance is tormented
by massacre, the murder of children.
This folly of noise and litter is Peace.

And what of you, tiniest of lives, that
wanders like a loose comma between lines?
Your apostrophe stillness endures
while the moon stares, the evening star shivers
and we scratch out our obituaries.

Roadside Festive

The bunting's out somewhere in Shropshire
below the Wrekin, in a layby
filled with low sun and an exotic tang
of bracken, rich, bucolic, friendly.

Uncle Reg stops the Hillman and we climb out
to stretch legs, empty overstretched bladders,
while our aunt unwraps spam sandwiches
from greaseproof paper, uncorks the Thermos.

There's coffee for the grown-ups, orange squash
for us. Far away across pine woods
the floating sun celebrates evening
as a bird wheezes out his strenuous song.

We rest in warm stillness, undream the world,
its *little bit of bread and no cheese*.

Ian Malcolm Parr

Names On The Wall

Some who lived here she knows. People
whose families grew. Walls they demolished,
turned beams to new uses, staircases shifted,
papered over ancient doors, the cracks of
lives. And hidden oak quietly acquired
its rot and worms. Peculiarities
covered for decades from interference.
She has stripped it bare.
All the years of tolerance, pink paint, soggy
carpets revealed, unveiling
stone, inelegant brickwork, broken mortar,
floorboards that cried when she removed
nails bloodied with dust. Each hand-forged twisted
iron treasure she counted into tin boxes.

Now she weeps with joists rotting in the yard.
Silently bids them goodbye.

Angels In The Hedgerows
Reflections on John Clare (1793-1864)

Ask if poets have such simple faith
and you reply in nightingales,
woodland and enclosures where
labouring people lived and starved.
Not all was beauty, not all impoverishment.
You paid our dues
leaving us a legacy poetry of the moment,
reflections in the clouds that crossed your mind.
Most of all you left us love.
A world better for your being,
garlands and pockets of song,
voices of birds, angels in the hedgerows,
saints who toiled in fields
they would never own.

Karen Schofield

Hope Valley

I laugh as wind and rain sting my face
at the top of Grindsbrook Clough,

rock forms are imagined shapes,
peat and gritstone underfoot.

Across a valley cut through by a railway line
Mam Tor shivers over Winnats pass

as stalactites grow drip by drip
in caverns underneath.

Purple heather on Stanage Edge
hugs us like a sweet, indifferent mother.

On the way to Burbage Bridge,
lambs and ewes cry, separated by a lane.

I walk hand in hand with the past,
hang on as tight as contours cling to Rushup Edge.

If I were on a train at Edale
approaching the Totley tunnel near the speed of light

time would slow, halt or delay
my own disordered path towards decay,

put on hold my cells' instructions,
revive a heart still scattered on Curbar Edge.

While the sun pours photons
reflected dappled green onto the Hope Valley.

Junior Doctor Learning Log
After Liz Berry

I have aimed bevelled needles between L3 and 4
and marvelled as spinal fluid fell drop by drop.

I have pierced arteries and countless veins,
watched cannulas fill with blood and saline flow,

worried about serum potassiums way too high
and puzzled over arterial gases when the pH was low.

I have recognised ST elevation on many ECGs
and spotted the pattern of atrial fibrillation

and listened to a thousand breaths in and out,
my stethoscope a fixture round my white coat.

I have watched the sunrise over hospital morgues
as the morning cast a cool light over my good works.

I have broken bad news and shared tears of grief
when there's no more to say and no need to speak

and turned away from results that shock
and learned when it's time to let a failing heart stop.

Myeloma Moths

The moths came with a soft flutter
one night and burrowed into
the deepest recesses of cloth.

Their offspring had their fill, gnawed
the wool and cashmere mix of a coat
framed by a hanger, shaped like you.

They punched out holes, some like stars
which didn't shine, coalesced into craters.
Silver dust littered the wardrobe carpet.

They were driven out, killed off a few times,
but younger generations grew,
attacked the arms, shoulders and back

until the coat was held together by threads.
Shrunken and spineless its days were numbered,
it shed bits of blue wool like tears.

Relativity At The Midnight Matinee

Seven Sisters twinkle in the autumn skies,
safe from Orion for eternity
for us to see. The end of a journey
through the vastness of space so long and far
their light set off as two star-crossed lovers
were created quill by quill, page by page.
And now we watch as actors tell their tale,
a tragedy unfolds, a doomed romance,
Juliet's wish for Romeo to be
cut into stars and pasted in the sky.
We see a constellation high above
while on the stage they've reached the final scene.
If we could we'd travel back in time, change
the ending, give us all a second chance.

John Smith

Tick All The Boxes

If it was alright, OK, suited me fine,
they told me to say that it ticked,
ticked all the boxes. So :

I ticked my tool box
for a spanner in their works,
my cool box for refreshment in the shade,
my cash box in case I made a hash
of it after all.

I ticked the gear box, eager for a change,
the fuse box, but found it on a trip.
My deed box, buried in a vault,
was ticked by proxy as an afterthought.

Next came the pill box, ticked
as an in-case-you're-ill box or
a long-ago I'm-here-to-kill-box.
The snuff box I ticked off for snorting
at the powder puff box Granny left behind
when her nose forgot to shine.

I ticked my tuck box till my luck like lemonade
ran out – the box ticked off to be 'First Aid'
proved to contain precisely nowt. So I ticked
the work box, basket case of pins and needles
but dropped a stitch and lost the thread and
ticked instead the had-enough-box that
in the States they call a casket.

So I ticked all the boxes like they said
and now I'm something that rhymes with bread
hoping that one day you'll find that little
black box I left behind. Prise it open
and you will find what made me TICK.

John Statham

Wake For Brown

I love my new clock with its old voice,
tock of the nursery rhymes,
tick of antique tales,
chimes of nostalgia –
not that pusillanimous fidget of quartz.

Not that I'm averse to a touch of the moderns:
see in me the maestro of the microwave,
king of the oven chip,
wizard of the telly zapper,
and renowned raconteur of answer-phone fame.

But there were two old-timers I had come to miss –
brown hair on my comb
and a wind-up clock.

Pity about the hair.

Not Waving

My goldfish in his goldfish bowl
must surely be a lonely soul
for watching people through the glass
he sees them stop and look and pass
and knows that he can never win
a passing friend and ask him in.

He also is a touch depressed
and carps a bit and shows unrest
because his postcode means he's spent
years in a closed environment.
He does what nature makes him do
then swims in it and drinks it too.

An Anthology

John Statham

One ray of light – he knows that he
can swim at peace, rely on me
to change his water, feed him food
and chat with him but not intrude.
Within his glassy universe
he's quiet but he could do worse –

no anglers, sharks, no prowling cats,
no forms to fill, no bureaucrats,
no violence and no persecution,
only his personal pollution.
While we have TV, oven chips,
computer games and battleships,
stripy ice-cream for desserts
and polyester in our shirts,
and nuclear waste and empty seas
and melting ice-caps, dying trees,
and fewer butterflies and birds,
too many mouths, too many words.

I think that on our spinning ball
we too will have no friends at all
if global warming boils us through
excessive burps of CO_2,
or rubbing out the ozone layer,
we fry because it isn't there.

Whichever, Mankind will at least
provide a cosmic gourmet's feast.
The menu will include no bread
but Homo Sapiens Soup instead,
and then, for plat du jour maybe
Fricassee of Humanity.

My goldfish in his goldfish bowl
will surely be a lonely soul;
no one to watch, no one to pass,
his water clouding in its glass,
no one to tell him that we went
and drowned in our own effluent.

Betty Titley

To A Brother

I struggle to absorb the words –
*last nigh*t *– feeding the calves – heart attack.*
My brain refuses to comprehend.
I call up your face, ruddy with sun and windburn,
stubbled with spiny black whiskers,
but with a white band on your forehead which,
out of doors, was always covered by an ancient cloth cap.
Hayseeds and chaff sprinkled in your hair.
You cannot be gone so suddenly from us.
This was your seventieth year, to be celebrated. All day,
as I speak of you to sisters and cousins and friends
I see the portrait photograph of you at three,
on a high stool, in velvet trousers, hair slicked,
your eyes alight with mischief, and your knees
pink and chubby …

Partings

We were five,
infants in Miss Hardy's class at the Endowed School,
on our way home for dinner; ten or so children
who lived in Upperthorpe. Ahead, the boys shouted and
   shoved,
the girls sauntered behind. The kerb was high,
the pavement narrow, the road steep. I remember
the whining grind of the lorry as it passed us and then
the sight of the driver in the road cradling Alan in his arms.
Most of my childhood memories are pictures, warm in
   colour,
gentle in tone. Alan's death is etched in acid on my brain.

*

Loving her, I become one with her will,
the will to be gone. To extinction? To heaven?
Who knows? Just to be gone from this hell.
My hand is clenched white-knuckled
on the bed frame, my back rigid with the effort
to help her open the gate of her prison.
As we wait for what becomes dad's last visit
she says fiercely *Don't let him hold me back.*

At the funeral I feel only thankfulness.
Joy even. It is months before I grieve.

Megan Smith

Undercurrent

Leviathan
rises slowly from the deep.
He surveys the landscape,
lifts his nose to the north,
eager for the smell of seal.
But there is nothing –
just a biting wind
and sheet-ice stretching out before him
for mile after mile.
He heaves his massive body
from the sea,
shaking the water
from his dense fur,
sending spray flying
into the air around him.
Driven by hunger, he moves on
across the empty waste –
disappears over the horizon.

Another Place
On seeing sculptor Antony Gormley's collection of 100 cast-iron men on Crosby Beach, Merseyside

Our eyes fixed
firmly on the horizon,
we the hundred,
reach out with our dreams
to new lands, new beginnings.
Though the draining sands
would turn us back,
we are resolute – stand firm
against the driving rain
and constant onslaught

of the wind and waves.
Naked – we carry nothing
but the hopes of all mankind,
held in our steady gaze
and the solid strength
of our silent forms.

Talking Of Socks

Red socks, white socks,
grey socks, black socks,
spotty socks, striped socks,
oh, so very pretty socks.

Lost socks, found socks,
comfy socks, itchy socks,
tight socks, stretchy socks,
always falling down socks.

Warm socks, woolly socks,
long socks, short socks,
bed socks, sports socks,
hole in the toe socks.

Odd socks, faded socks,
darned socks, frayed socks,
much loved faded socks,
couldn't throw away socks.

Forever

We are true friends
you and I,
constant companions.
I was drawn to you
from the beginning.
I have climbed your hills
and walked in your valleys.
I have known your warmth
in the morning sun,
and the bitter cold of you
in winter snow.
You were always there –
firm and sure
beneath my feet.
You were there with me
as I took my first faltering steps.
You will be there at my end
to enfold me –
hold me – for all time.

Annabel Wade

Gannets Off Port Soy

Often, they spike through my mind with their ice-pick
beaks, take off in my dreams on their enormous
wings. The gannets thrum their black and white
feathers across the sky, the sea cracks on the rocks
at the harbour entrance. So many birds flocking and

climbing on this wild day when the clouds are steaming,
they possess the air, are incredible in glides and turns.
Their binocular eyes scan the mint sea, they are focused
and precise as surgery. One by one they point their bodies,
plunge accurate as a scalpel into the waves. Just for a
  moment

they are at the edge of two worlds liminal and god-like
they pierce the underworld and are transfigured into
iridescent sea creatures. The shoals are serene in their
  oceanic
heaven, the gannets shock through the silence. Now

with a explosion of wings they resurrect like vicious
angels and become air again while ice pearls
drop from their feathers. The herring are sacrificed,
the gannets' yellow heads catch fire in the sun.

Child

Your heart is a freshly painted room
so tender I can hardly bear it

See how empty it is with the windows
flung open to welcome every breeze

Smelling so sweetly with its white walls
and soft rugs in which the feet can sink

I long to catch the arrows of your future
so they never turn your white room red

Kintsugi

See this shattered vase,
the Zen master reverently
turns each shard with tender fingers.

In his expert eye he patiently
cradles each broken piece,
loving every flaw.

He mixes the gold,
fills the cracks until they gleam,
recreates a rarity and beauty.

He knows every fracture
is a sharp edge of loss
that cannot be disguised.

The vase glows, is resurrected
shattered, damaged and fragile
not mended but transfigured.

Scottish Image

There is no pollution here.
Trees thick with lichen
pattern sunlight through their trunks,
only our boots heavy on the track
invade the ancient woodland.

As we emerge from the forest
a mountain shocks with brightness,
a vista stretches lazy as an August day.
The hills are green and gold, calm in the morning air.
The horizon winks with seductive water,
from here the breath can mingle with the sea.

I grab my camera
to shoot this moment
to trap and trophy it
but the lens and I lose focus
the camera sneers, 'Battery Low'.
I cannot cull a single frame
the camera dies in my hand.

A swallow zooms at the edge of the wind.
The air glitters, the day is free.
A butterfly flashes through thistle and cornflower.
My breath is filled with light and peace and knowing
I surrender to the moment,
the image slowly develops in my heart.

Mary Williams

Pickling Onions

She shucked off their crisp skins,
wielding the knife.
Topped and tailed them,
undid their overcoats.

But while she was crying the sacrifice of tears
they became
brown flakey eyeballs in the bowl,
(soaked to extract the pungent caramel dye)
and then her tears abated.
She had won.

Skinned and naked,
bobbing in the bowl of salty brine
they waited, pressed into jars.

Later, vinegar drenched and wedged,
they have no pity for her.

She walks into the larder
and rows of jars
watch her with vinegar eyes.

Her hands need washing.

Tracklements (A Lancashire Memory)

It were nobbut meat-and-tater pie
she gave us. Her up at t'school cooked it
in reet big pan wi' pastry crust.

There were a crowd that neet,
wi' lads on bikes from over Barnoldswick,
all of 'em clemmed and code.
Gobbiners from up t'valley,
they was wanting pie.

Tracklements we asked for, wi' it,
to make it tasty, like.
Then she got red cabbage oot.
Weel! That were it then.
Red cabbage, vinegared,
a bittee sauce … Ay,
we was well suited.

Can't have meat and tater pie
wi' no tracklements, eh, lad?

An' gi' us wallies, onions, pickles in't jar.

Summat to make us teeth itch.
Summat to tell us we're alive.
Tracklements.
Ay, it were good,
reet good,
wi' a noggin o'Thwaites
to wash it down
and plenty tracklements.
You should'a come!

Philip Williams

Uniform
i.m. Edward William Bennett M.C. (1895-1970)

My wife remembered your dislocated
grind and click at mealtimes; childhood alarm
as you lifted your jaw to slot it back in place.
Her mother recalled the raw gap between
neck and shoulder as you dug or washed,
that eerie absence where the flesh had been.
The surgeons took a final shot before
they sent you home, proud of their trade, so keen
to pass their methods on. Three-quarters turned,
scar tissue tucked shipshape beneath lapels,
you peer from each family mantelpiece,
buttoned tight, belted tight, your uniform
airbrushed neat on their sepia prints,
sleek as your slicked back hair, your collar
folded then sucked in slightly, like a sail.

Perennials
i.m. Penelope (Penny) Anne Williams, 1962-2018

Wind tugs frayed twine across each raised bed,
bends the broken stems of this year's seedlings,
wafts wigwam-ties the coal-tits tear and peck
to line their nests. They must feel it raw,
two men on the roof opposite, all boots
and tar and builder's bums. They stand and stretch,
chafe in the heat they've poured to seal the gaps.
I prod, hoe, bend to fill a trug with weeds.
Our shared copper beech rustles, nods and stirs.

I will wild this garden, blur the verges but retain
your borders, those deft perennials you planted:
foxglove, iris, clematis, forget-me-nots –
thread through all your cream varieties of rose,
the one you ordered for its name, The Poet's Wife.

Red Triangle

Some things have their own signs –
workmen, deer, horse-drawn vehicles, ice.
Highways red-edge their warnings for us,
gradients, uneven roads, hump backed bridge.
Road-bound life is black and white,
block-stamped cars that queue or skid,
one that plunges clear across a quayside ledge.

Even toads have their own, a black blot
on a white ground, warts specked out,
wet glint in rain or halogen beam.
A swing-bridge pivots above ruffled waves,
a wind-sock flutters in a side wind.
Beware low flying aircraft, children,
elderly who prod across the road with sticks.

Some things give little warning –
a longer quietness in the traffic queue,
infrequent visits, unanswered texts,
fresh gossip beside the water-cooler.
We miss pangs, hints, cut corners, hurtle through
shared silences between work and sleep,
topple into stillness as the engine stops.

One Long Summer

An early chill. Gran' buoys us to the beach
to bear the cold. Great Uncle Eric clashes
gears, revs his vexed Land Rover awake
to drag caravans up steep-sided Cornish lanes.
He's as stiff-backed at the wheel as Gran's
intent on our stinging dip before the beaches fill.
We teeter over bladder-wrack to the arched outcrop
where they've cemented off a rock pool from the sea.
Gran plunges in, all round in her one-piece, her stout limbs
  spread
with goose-fat, head-down, breasting back and forth.
The trapped sea's sharp salt-slap jolts us both to life:
sudden 'hereness' of skin and pores, beat of blood
beneath the scalp, breath-burn between the ribs,
pound and churn about our ears.

There will be time to watch the hermit-crab,
the sea-anemones' pink pout and wink,
to poke at dog-fish egg-cases with sticks.

For now, there's Gran, oaring her gritty bulk from
rock face to limpet-studded concrete wall
in our sealed tight slice of sea. Her dogged strokes
she hopes will train us to confront life head-on,
arms flexed to sweep all aside and pull us through.
Frog-spread kick and thrust behind. Never mind the cold.

Acknowledgements

All of Hilary Adams' poems appeared in *Slantwise Sometimes*; 'Bedtime Stories' Part 1 previously appeared in *Total Recall*.

Rosemary Brough's 'Letting It Go' and 'The Terrace, Penkhull' were first published in *The Reader*.

Caroline Hawkridge's 'Peregrine' was Highly Commended in the York Open Poetry competition 2010 and first published in *The Dark Horse*; thanks to Derby Cathedral's Peregrine Project, derbyperegrines.blogspot.com/; 'Cockerel' was originally published in *The Interpreter's House;* 'Saqqara' was originally published in *Shearsman*.

Both Roger Hill's poems appeared in his 2017 collection, *The Snow Coin*.

Helen Kay's 'Friday Afternoons Are Different Now' was runner-up in the 2023 Wirral Festival poetry competition; 'Lighting The Wood Stove Six Months After Your Death' won the Leeds Peace Poetry Prize 2024.

Bill Milner's 'Home' From *This Colder Room*, Woodlands Press, 2013; 'The Garden from Daybreak', Woodlands Press, 2010.

Harry Owen's 'Message From Astbury Mere' from *Searching for Machynlleth*, NPF, 2000.

Ian Malcolm Parr's 'Angels In The Hedgerows' from *Singing Tomorrows*, Cestrian Press.

Both Karen Schofield's 'Junior Doctor Learning Log' and 'Myeloma Moths' were commended in The Hippocrates Prize and published by The Hippocrates Press; 'Myeloma Moths' appeared in the 2019 edition of *Tools of the Trade: Poems for New Doctors*, Scottish Poetry Library, and 'Junior Doctor Learning Log' in the 2022 edition; 'Relativity At The Midnight Matinee' was first published online in *Consilience* – audio available at: https://soundcloud.com/user-130643584/relativity-at-the-midnight.

John Smith's 'Tick All The Boxes' from *Keele Haul*, 2012.

John Statham's 'Not Waving' from *Doodling With Venus*, 2000.

Annabel Wade's 'Gannets Off Port Soy' first published in *Keele Haul*, 2012.

Philip Williams' 'Red Triangle' long-listed for the National Poetry Competition and Commended in the Sentinel Poetry Competition 2019.

www.ingramcontent.com/pod-product-compliance
Lightning Source LLC
Chambersburg PA
CBHW051552010526
44118CB00022B/2678